HOW TO WATCH
CRICKET

John

with

Former England Captain

Mike Denness

Illustrated by **Bill Tidy**

Foreword by **Dickie Bird** M.B.E.

Published in 1994 by
Uptonia Ltd
Tectonic Place
Holyport Road
Maidenhead
Berkshire SL6 2YG

ISBN 0 7522 0877 2

Foreword

by
Dickie Bird M.B.E

Dickie Bird has umpired over 50 Test matches and also nearly 100 one-day internationals, including three World Cup Finals. All these achievements are world records. He is known, loved and respected throughout the world of cricket.

This book is ideal for for anyone new to cricket who wants to know how to enjoy watching the game.

It explains the game very clearly.

In fact, I think that even experienced cricket lovers will find it worth reading. It reminds us why cricket is a unique and a wonderful game.

Mike Denness, as England Captain, has seen and played the game at the highest level.

John Hatch, my fellow Yorkshireman, knows the grass-roots appeal of the game to the village cricketer and to those who just want to watch.

Mike Denness and John Hatch were recently with me, and watching, in Zimbabwe and New Zealand, when I was very proud to be the 'international' Test match umpire first in a pilot scheme and then in the official launch of the National Grid International Panel. The authors have played a big role, with the International Cricket Council, in helping to raise umpiring standards, and also the status of umpires, around the world.

I was very pleased to be asked to provide the foreword to this book. It is very helpful and I recommend it to everyone who watches cricket.

Dickie Bird M.B.E.
April 1994

A FOUR

A SIX

BYES

LEG BYES

WIDE

CAN'T HEAR YOU

NO BALL

DEAD
BALL

OUT

Introduction

Welcome to the game of cricket!

A Brief Outline

Let's start with a brief outline of the game.

Cricket is played on a large field by two teams of 11 players. In the middle of the field is a pitch with two wickets, 22 yards apart.

The two teams take it in turn to bat and score runs. Whilst one team is batting the other team is bowling and fielding.

Only two players bat at any one time – in a partnership. The other nine players in the batting team sit in the pavilion and watch them. When one of the batsman is out he is replaced by another – until ten batsmen have been out and the team's innings is completed.

The side that is bowling and fielding has all of its 11 players on the field.

One player in the fielding side bowls a cricket ball at whichever batsman is facing. If the batsman hits the ball (with his bat) the two batsmen can score runs for their side by running between the wickets, to change ends, before the fielding side can retrieve the ball. Runs are also scored if the ball crosses the boundary of the field.

The main objective of the game is to score more runs than the opposition.

Two Versions of the Game

There are two versions of Cricket. There is the traditional game and a variation called the limited-overs' game (or, popularly, one-day cricket).

The first match that you watch may well be a limited-overs' game.

The Traditional Game

At the top level, the traditional game is played over several days. An international game (a Test match) is normally played over five days, with six hours of play on each day. Within this playing time, each team is entitled to have two innings.

In the traditional game the result can be a draw – where neither side wins or loses.

The game is drawn unless one side (the loser) has completed its two innings and the other side (the winner) has scored more runs. In other words, a team cannot win a (traditional) game merely by scoring more runs. The opposition must also have completed its two innings.

This has a big influence on tactics. A team that is well behind on runs may be able to avoid defeat by batting out time for a draw. To counter this, a team that is well ahead on runs may declare its innings closed to give it more time to get the opposition out.

Limited-Overs

In a limited-overs' game each team has only one innings. The innings must close, even though less than ten batsmen have been out, when a set number of balls have been bowled. (In practice, the limit is described in terms of overs and not balls. An over consists of six balls. Overs are bowled alternately from each end of the pitch.) The permitted number of overs is normally 50 in an international match. In other matches it may be 40, 50, 55 or 60).

Whichever team scores the most runs in its innings is the winner. The match therefore cannot end in a draw. (If both teams score the exact same number of runs, which is most unusual, the result is a tie).

Limited-overs' cricket has become increasingly popular in recent years. The main reason is that spectators can go for the day and (weather permitting) will see both sides bat and bowl with a definite result to the game. The World Cup (first played in 1975) is a limited-overs' competition.

In some limited-overs' competitions (including, now, the World Cup) the two teams wear coloured clothing rather than the traditional white. The traditional red ball is then replaced by a white ball. A white ball is essential if the game is played under floodlights in day/night matches (see page 62). A red ball is standard only because cricket balls are normally made with (tough) brown leather which can most easily be dyed red to make them more visible (in daylight). It should also be remembered that, in the 18th and 19th centuries, players normally wore items of coloured clothing – so white is not quite so traditional as many people now assume.

Watching on TV

TV is particularly good for close-ups and for action replays. TV sets are increasingly available, at the ground, in boxes and around bars. In addition some grounds have big screens which show replays.

However, if you always stay at

ome to watch on TV, you will obviously miss much of the atmosphere at the ground. That said, much better TV than nothing and cricket gets good coverage.

At the Ground

To get into the ground you will need a ticket. Some international matches, and the finals of domestic limited-overs' competitions, are very popular and tickets are sold long in advance.

If you are lucky, perhaps someone will invite you as a guest. Or a friend may be able to tell you how you can buy a ticket. Otherwise, you can find out about tickets by telephoning the ground where the game is to be played. The number will be in the phone book. (Try looking under 'Sports Clubs' if you don't know which club normally plays at the ground.)

Where to sit is normally not all that important as regards the view. You can watch cricket enjoyably from anywhere in the ground.

Some people like to sit as directly as possible behind the bowler's arm, where they can see whether the ball is swinging through the air or deviating off the pitch. However, if you do sit here

be very careful not to move when the bowling is from your end. Movement can distract the batsman and he might, very publicly, hold up play until you settle down!

Another favoured position is square to the pitch, where you can see how quickly the ball is travelling and also get a good view of any run-outs.

A more practical consideration is that in some parts of the ground you will find that your neighbours are relatively sedate; in other parts they will seem more boisterous. This is a matter of personal preference.

If you sitting are in the sun, without shelter, you should wear a hat. You will probably be able to buy one at the ground.

H. NIBLOE & Co
PRIVATE

First Impressions at the Ground

You have shown your ticket at the gate and you are now in your seat.

On your way in, did you notice:

the picnic hampers?

the various hats?

the brightly coloured striped ties (many worn by respectable-looking elderly gentlemen)?

the youngsters wearing the same shirts as the players?

You may also have noticed that quite a lot of spectators are women – a growing and very welcome influence on the game.

But let's look at the field of play. What do you see?

For a start (unless the game is part of one of the special competitions where the two teams wear different coloured clothing) you will notice that everyone on the field is dressed in white – except for two men wearing white coats and black trousers.

If you were to count up, you would see 15 people altogether.

The two in white coats and black trousers are the **umpires**. They are not players. They are in charge of the game.

One umpire will be standing by something called a **wicket**; but which for the moment looks like a yellow and elongated letter 'm'.

The other umpire will be standing about 30 yards to the side of another wicket.

The other 13 people on the field are players.

You will see that three of the players are wearing pads on their legs.

Two of these will also be holding bats. They are the **batsmen** and members of the batting side. (All the other players on the field are members of the fielding side).

One of the batsmen will be standing by the wicket near the umpire – holding his bat in one hand and watching. The other batsman will be standing by the other wicket – and holding his bat in both hands ready to hit the ball. The third player wearing pads is the **wicket-keeper**. He is a key member of the fielding side. He will be wearing a pair of big gloves and he will probably be standing quite a long way behind the wicket at which the batsman is preparing to receive the ball.

Most of the other players (nine to be exact) will be **fielders**. Those who are closest to the batting wicket will crouch down when something seems about to happen. The rest of the fielders, who are further away, will walk in

A FIELDER

THE WICKET KEEPER

THE BATSMAN

A FIELDER

A FIELDER

THE BOWLER

A PIGEON

THE UMPIRE

towards the batsman as the **bowler** starts to run up.

The bowler?

The bowler is the player you will notice most. You will see him run up to the wicket (near the umpire) and, with a sort of windmill action, he will hurl the ball down towards the batsman at the far end. He will (normally) make the ball bounce before it reaches the batsman. He will do this six times. Then another member of the fielding side will bowl six times from the other wicket; then back again and so on. Six balls make an **over**. Overs are bowled alternatively from each wicket.

Some of the balls will go straight through to the wicket-keeper; with the batsman perhaps lifting his bat high in the air to let the ball pass.

Some of the balls may hit the batsman on his pads; and there may be shouts from the fielders.

The batsman may hit some of the balls with his bat; merely to stop them.

Sometimes the batsman will hit the ball and, while a fielder retrieves it, the two batsmen will run towards each other, cross, and change ends. (You will then see some of the numbers change on a large scoreboard).

Very occasionally, there will be loud shouts, an umpire will raise his finger to a roar from the crowd, and one of the batsman (who is out) will slowly walk off the field to be replaced by another.

So what is the point of it all? Why is this a game that some people treat almost as if it were a religion?

More specifically, how can a new spectator hope to understand enough about cricket to enjoy watching it?

The answer is really quite easy. Just turn the page and read on!

The Basics of Cricket

Let's now restart by looking at baseball and rounders.

Baseball and rounders are games in which a batsman hits a ball and **runs**.

Both games are played by two teams who take it in turn to try to score runs.

The winning team is the one which has scored the most runs when the losing team has completed all its **innings**.

In baseball and rounders the ball is thrown through the air at the batsman. The batsman scores a run by hitting the ball and then running from base to base until he reaches home.

The fielders try to get the batsman **out – caught** (by catching the ball from the hit before it touches the ground) or **run out** (by getting the ball to a base before the batsman reaches it).

Cricket is also a game in which two teams take it in turn to try to hit the ball and score runs. The batsmen can also be caught or run out.

However, cricket has two very important differences from baseball and rounders.

We need to understand what these two important differences are.

BOWLED OUT

AN IMPORTANT
DIFFERENCE...

First Important Difference

The Wicket/Bowled Out

In cricket, unlike baseball, the batsman is not out because he fails to hit the ball. Instead, he can be **out, bowled.**

In cricket there are two **wickets**, 22 yards apart, at each end of the **pitch**.

Each wicket is made up of three (equal-sized) wooden **stumps** with two wooden **bails** resting on top. Each wicket is nine inches wide and 28 inches high.

The wicket is **broken** (or **down**) if one, or both, of the bails is dislodged.

If the **bowler delivers a ball**, fairly, which hits and breaks the wicket (dislodges a bail) the batsman is out, bowled.

Sometimes, when a batsman is bowled, not just the bails but also a stump goes flying through the air. This adds to the spectacle and excitement; but has no other significance.

The important thing is that, in cricket, the batsman has to think about more than just hitting the ball and scoring runs. Whilst he would obviously like to score runs, he also has to be careful that he doesn't miss a ball on the wicket and be bowled.

In cricket, the batsman therefore has to think about **defence** as well as **attack**.

THE BALL BOUNCES

AN IMPORTANT DIFFERENCE...

OR THE BALL HITS YOU!

Second Important Difference

Bouncing Ball/'Straight Bat'

In cricket, the bowler (normally) makes the ball bounce before it reaches the batsman. A ball that bounces awkwardly is generally more difficult to hit than a **full toss** (or **full pitch**).

(If you don't believe this, just imagine trying to play a baseball or rounders shot at a ball that bounces a yard in front of your feet!)

This has a very important consequence.

The best way to hit a ball that bounces awkwardly is to hold the bat vertically (with the handle at the top and the blade of the bat underneath). In this way the batsman can get his head (and eyes) behind the **line** of the ball and judge its position.

When the batsman is playing with the bat vertical he is said to be playing with a **straight bat**. Otherwise he is playing with a **cross bat**.

The batsman playing with a straight bat is the hallmark of cricket.

Notice, however, a snag in holding the bat vertically. This makes it easier to stop a bouncing ball but it also makes it more difficult to hit the ball very hard.

The more natural way to swing a bat, to make a good hard hit, it to swing it horizontally, as a baseball player does.

The batsman, in cricket, therefore has to choose, with every ball, between playing the type of shot which is most effective in:

- simply stopping a bouncing ball, which might hit the wicket;

or

- giving the ball a good hard hit (if he manages to make contact)

Notice that in cricket, unlike baseball, the batsman does not have to run if he hits the ball. He can play a defensive shot and stay where he is.

STRAIGHT BAT

CROSS BAT

PLAYING FOR A DRAW

Cricket versus Baseball

In cricket, the batsman must protect the wicket to avoid being bowled.

In cricket, the ball can bounce awkwardly. To have a reasonable chance of making contact, the batsman may have to play the ball with a straight bat rather than a cross bat.

With every ball he receives, the batsman must therefore decide whether:

to play an attacking shot (to score runs); or

to play a defensive shot (to protect his wicket); or

to leave the ball alone.

(The batsman may also deliberately allow the ball to hit his pads. We will see later, when we eventually look at all the ways of getting out, that a batsman can sometimes protect his wicket by putting his pads in the way. In some cases he will be given out if he does this; but in other cases he may either be entitled to stop the ball with his pads or he may get the benefit of any doubt as to whether the ball would have hit the wicket).

If the batsman decides to play an attacking shot he must then choose between playing with a straight bat and a cross bat.

Cricket is therefore a more complex game than baseball.

Another difference between traditional cricket and baseball is that a game of cricket can end in a draw where neither side wins.

However this applies only to the traditional version of cricket. The limited-overs' version of cricket is specifically designed to eliminate the draw.

In other words, the limited-overs' version of cricket makes the game a little more similar to baseball – shorter to play and producing an outright winner.

THE BATSMEN RUNNING

Scoring Runs

Let's now look at the actual way that runs are scored in cricket.

In cricket, the two wickets also serve as the bases for running.

In cricket there are always two (and only two) batsmen **in** at any one time. One of these batsman is called the **striker**. He is the batsman who happens to be **facing** the bowling. He obviously stands in a position where he can protect the wicket that is being bowled at.

The other batsman is called the **non-striker**. He stands near the other wicket while the bowler bowls.

The batsmen get a run if, after the ball has been delivered, they change ends before the fielders can retrieve the ball and use it to break one of the wickets (dislodge a bail) and run out one of the batsmen. If the batsman manage to change ends twice they get two runs, and so on.

To avoid being run out a batsman must **make his ground** by getting his bat, or some part of his person, behind **the batting crease** which is a marked line four feet in front of each wicket. The batsman is **in his ground** if he has some part of his body or his bat (provided, of course, that he is holding his bat) **grounded** behind the back edge of the batting crease. Otherwise the batsman is **out of his ground**.

(Notice here that the bat must be on the ground. It is no good the batsman just waving it in the air behind the batting crease. This is why you will see batsmen run the bat along the ground in front of them if they think they are in danger of being run out).

If the batsman is out of his ground he can be **run out** by a fielder (including the wicket-keeper) breaking the wicket. The fielder may break the wicket either with the ball or with his hand whilst he is holding the ball (in the same hand).

There is also another way of scoring runs. The batsmen have no need to run between the wickets if the ball crosses the **boundary** of the playing area. This is called **a boundary**; and four runs are scored automatically. Four runs becomes six runs if the ball is hit over the boundary without it bouncing.

A boundary is therefore called either a **four** or a **six**; depending upon whether the ball has bounced before it crosses the boundary.

(Notice, by the way, that the laws of cricket do not specify any particular dimensions for the boundaries of the playing area. In Test matches (i.e. international matches) the boundaries need to

OVERTHROWS

be reasonably far away from the wickets. A distance of about 80 yards (from the nearest wicket) seems to give a reasonable balance between the batsmen's chances to hit sixes and the fielders' chances to take catches. However, even Test match rounds all have slightly differently shaped playing areas. This adds to the charm of the game).

Runs for the Batsman

All runs scored are added to the batting team's total.

However, the **scorers** also keep a careful record of which batsman has hit the ball because in the score book (and on the scoreboard), each batsman is credited with his own personal tally which contributes to the team's total.

It makes no difference to the result of the **match** which particular batsman happens to score the runs for his team. In practice, however, everyone is always very interested to know the individual scores of each batsmen.

Extras

The batting team can also score **extras**. These count towards the team's total but not to any batsman's individual score.

If the striker has completely missed the ball, the batsmen can still run for **byes** if the wicket keeper has also missed it (or fumbled it).

The batsmen can also run for **leg byes** if the ball has hit the batsman's body and has been deflected out of immediate reach of the fielders.

For leg byes, however, the batsman must have been attempting either to play a shot or to dodge out of the way of the ball. The batsman cannot deliberately let the ball hit him and then take a run after the deflection. (If the batsmen ignore this, and try to run, the umpire will call **dead ball** and make them return to their original positions).

The batting team also automatically gets an extra run, under extras, if the bowler bowls either a **wide** or a **no ball** (see page 47).

Overthrows

Finally, the batsmen can run for **overthrows**. These can occur when the fielding side has retrieved the ball but has overthrown a wicket when attempting to return it. Overthrows count as runs for the batsman or as extras; whichever applies.

BAD LIGHT

RAIN STOPPED PLAY

The Innings

The batting side continues to bat until ten batsmen have been out (or ten **wickets have fallen**). Notice that although each team has eleven players only ten need to be dismissed to close the innings. This is because there must always be two batsmen in at the wicket.

In limited-overs' games, the innings will close, in any case, when the agreed maximum number of overs have been bowled.

In traditional cricket, a captain can **declare** an innings closed if he thinks his team has scored enough runs and he wants time to bowl the opposition out.

Interruptions to Play

The players sometimes come off the field because of weather interruptions.

'Rain stopped play' means exactly that. So does 'bad light stopped play'. Interruptions are frustrating to spectators but cricket is played with a hard ball, about the same size as a tennis ball, that can travel very fast. To avoid injury, let alone play with skill, the players need to be able to see the ball clearly. The main problem with rain is that it makes the ground (and the ball) slippery.

Bowling, fielding, batting and running between the wickets all become dangerous in slippery conditions. For this reason, 'rain' can stop play for longer than it actually falls if it makes the ground wet and slippery.

It is normally up to the umpires to decide if conditions are fit for play. However, if both captains agree to carry on playing they may.

If a traditional game is interrupted by bad weather the game resumes where it left off. In a limited-overs' game, however, the playing conditions often specify that the number of overs will be reduced if playing time is lost. If this adjustment has to be made while the game is in progress it usually penalises one side unfairly by altering the balance of overs, runs and wickets. However, no-one has yet devised a workable adjustment formula which seems fair in all eventualities.

(Even the alternative, of providing a 'reserve day' to make up the lost time, has its drawbacks. The playing conditions may change significantly overnight. More to the point, most of the spectators will miss the end of the game if it goes over into the next day).

- The score is 247 for 6 wickets.
- Batsman No. 3 has scored 102; batsman No. 8 has scored 8.
- The last batsman was out for 23 when the score was 214.
- There have been 10 extras in the innings.
- Bowlers Nos. 10 and 9 are bowling.
- 82 overs have been bowled in the innings (the new ball is nearly due – after 85 overs).

- 73 more overs must be bowled in the day (to reach 90 overs).
- In the first innings, the Home Team made 235. The Visitors replied with 350; a first innings lead of 115. The Home Team are therefore 132 runs ahead with four wickets remaining (not good!)
- Fielder No. 6 has just fielded the ball (top of scoreboard).

The Scoreboard

The state of the game is shown on a scoreboard. (At big grounds there are two; so every spectator can see at least one of them).

One of the real oddities of cricket is that no two scoreboards ever seem to be exactly alike! Also, most scoreboards seem to be a jumble of figures until you have worked out what is shown where. It is well worth doing this.

Look first for the total of the side that is batting. This number obviously increases every time a run, or an extra, is scored.

Look next for the number of wickets that have fallen. You then have the score e.g. 95 for 1; or 247 for 6; or whatever. (Australians tend to say the score the other way round e.g. 1 for 95; or 6 for 247).

Look next for the individual scores of the two current batsmen. Each batsman may be identified by name; or merely by a number (which you can get from a printed score-card available at the ground; or by asking your neighbour). A light often shows which batsman is the striker.

Another number will show the current total of extras.

The current bowlers will also be indicated (by name or number); and the scoreboard may also show how many overs they have each bowled (and perhaps, but not always, how many wickets they have each taken for how many runs scored off them).

The scoreboard may also show which player has just fielded the ball, often by showing a light against his number of the score-card.

The score made by the **last man** will be shown; and also the side's score at the fall of the **last wicket** (when he was out). The scoreboard may also show how he was out and who was the bowler. (Some scoreboards show these details for all the batsmen who have been out).

The scoreboard will also show the scores made by each side in its previous innings (if any).

Finally, the scoreboard will show the number of overs that have been bowled in the innings. (However, beware! In a Test match, played over several days this number will sometimes suddenly change to show the number of overs since the second new ball was taken [see page 55]). In addition, another number will say how may overs remain to be bowled during the day's play in order to reach the daily minimum of 90 overs. However, this number may also change suddenly if there is a change of innings (when the number has to be re-calculated).

RIGHT HANDED
BATSMAN

OFFSIDE   LEGSIDE

LEFT HANDED
BATSMAN

LEGSIDE   OFFSIDE

Batting

Right-handers and Left-handers

The batsman can bat either **right-handed** or **left-handed** as he chooses.

A right-handed batsman is one who holds the bat with his right hand lower on the handle. (The grip is similar to holding a tennis racket). The bottom hand gives most of the power to a shot and this is the natural method for people who are naturally right-handed.

The right-handed batsman's left hand goes near the top of the bat handle. (Imagine a left-handed table-tennis player playing a backhand shot.) The top hand is used mainly to help control the shot.

The batsman's grip is different from a golfer's grip because, in cricket, the two hands do not interlock.

A left-handed batsman, by contrast, holds the bat with his left hand lower on the handle and his right hand near the top.

Notice that as the bowler runs in to bowl he will see a right-handed batsman standing to the right of the wicket (as the bowler sees it) or a left-handed batsman standing to the left of the wicket.

Legside (or Onside) and Offside

If we draw an imaginary line, from wicket to wicket down the middle of the pitch, the side of the playing area in which the batsman has his legs is called the **legside** (or **onside**). The **offside** is the other side.

Which is the legside, and which is the offside, of the field therefore depends entirely on whether the batsman who is the striker is right-handed or left-handed; and therefore where he has his legs. There is no mystery to it!

FORWARD DEFENSIVE

BACKWARD DEFENSIVE

Batting

Defensive Shots

All defensive shots (to protect the wicket) are played with a straight bat (with the bat held vertically and with the batsman's head and eyes behind the line of the ball).

There are really only two defensive shots.

The **forward defensive** is where the batsman **plays forward** (i.e. stretches forward) and puts his weight on his front foot.

Alternatively, the batsman can defend **on the back foot**. In this case the batsman **plays back** and puts his weight on his back foot.

In both cases, the batsman intends to stop the ball rather than to hit it hard.

The batsman will also try to play the ball down to the ground. If the ball goes up in the air the batsman is likely to be caught by one of the fielders.

The batsman keeps the ball down by keeping his top hand on the bat in front of his bottom hand. This angles the face of the bat downwards.

(Notice that if the batsman has his bottom hand in front of his top hand he will spoon the ball upwards and probably get caught out. He can then be said to have 'cocked it up' or to have 'made a cock up'. This is an old cricketing expression – it appeared 50 years ago in a cricket coaching manual written by the legendary Yorkshire and England batsman Herbert Sutcliffe, who was noted for his impeccable manners – but the expression tends not to be used in the game nowadays).

THE DRIVE

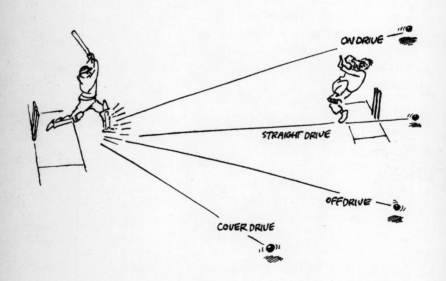

ON DRIVE

STRAIGHT DRIVE

OFFDRIVE

COVER DRIVE

Batting

Attacking Shots – Straight Bat

Some attacking shots are also played with a straight bat.

The most elegant attacking shot is the **drive**. The ball is hit in front of the batsman.

The drive is played against a ball known as a **half-volley**. This is a ball that bounces conveniently for the batsman by coming straight onto the **meat of the bat**. (Hitting a half volley is rather similar to making a drop-kick in rugby; in both cases the ball gets clouted shortly after it bounces off the ground).

The **cover drive** is the most beautiful shot in cricket. The ball skims off at about 45 degrees to the batsman's **offside**. It is played by **opening the face of the bat** (i.e. twisting the wrists around slightly) as the ball is stuck.

The **off drive** goes straighter, but still on the offside.

The **straight drive** goes straight back down the pitch

The **on drive** goes to **the legside** (or **onside**).

A drive is normally played with the batsman's weight on the front foot. However, a skilful player can also drive off the back foot.

A drive can also be played to a low full toss. The ball has to be in the same position that it would have been if it had bounced and been a half-volley.

A top class batsman can also **clip the ball off his legs** so that it goes either side of **square** on the legside. This shot is played with a straight bat and is very difficult to play. (The shot is also called a **whip**.)

The **glance** (or **leg glance**) is a deflection behind the batsman on his legside. It is also played with a straight bat. The batsman lets the ball come on to him as if to play a defensive shot; then **closes** the face of the bat (i.e. turns it with his wrists) at the moment of impact with the ball. The turn of the wrists at the last moment converts the shot from a defensive stroke to one that produces runs.

The glance can be very effective against fast, and fast medium, bowlers because the ball speeds away towards the boundary with no real effort from the batsman. We shall see later that when a fast, or fast medium, bowler is bowling, the fielding side (almost) always places one of its fielders on the boundary to stop glances going for fours.

CUTS, PULLS AND HOOKS

CUT   PULL   HOOK

Batting

Attacking Shots – Horizontal Bat

If the ball is outside the off-stump, and has bounced conveniently (so the batsman has time to judge its height), the batsman may be able to hit it away with a horizontal bat.

The **cut** is played with a horizontal bat to a ball on the offside. The bat is brought down on the ball which is hit more or less, square to the offside.

A **late cut** is played as the ball passes the batsman on the offside and it sends the ball behind the batsman, on the offside. The ball is dabbed down and the shot needs very little force.

The other shots played with a horizontal bat are used for balls on the legside or even on the wicket. The ball needs to bounce conveniently (so the batsman has time to judge its height).

The **pull** is played with a horizontal bat to the legside. It is not quite the same as a baseball shot because the batsman normally pulls by **getting in line** with the ball and hitting it square to the legside.

The **hook** is similar to the pull except that the batsman gets **inside the line** of the ball and hits it behind him on the legside. The hook is used to a ball that has bounced up around the batsman's head.

The **sweep** is also played with a horizontal bat to the legside; but the batsman goes down on one knee. The sweep is played only against **spin** bowling (i.e. not against fast or fast medium bowling). The ball is hit just before or just after it bounces; with the bat held more or less at full stretch down the wicket. The ball goes behind the wicket on the legside.

(The **reverse sweep** is a fancy shot sometimes used in limited-overs' games. The batsman reverses the face of the bat and sweeps the ball behind the wicket on the off-side).

DID NOT INTEND

Batting

Other Shots

Not all scoring shots can be strictly defined. Many a run is scored because the ball hits the edge of the bat and flies off in a direction that the batsman did not intend.

Sometimes a batsman may deliberately create a similar effect by flicking a short-pitched and high-bouncing ball behind him to the offside, over the heads of the **slip** fielders (see page 53). Alternatively, the batsman may **steer** the ball down the **third man** (see page 55) by angling his bat to the offside and playing the ball down. This shot is common in limited-overs' cricket when there are no slip fielders.

A forward defensive stroke can sometimes become more of a **push** which goes for a single (or even, with perfect timing, a four).

If you watch carefully, you will also, quite often, see a batsman driving at a ball with his bat quite a long way out of the vertical (so that the stroke becomes more like a golf shot). This tends to happen if the ball is wider to the offside than the batsman had expected. If the batsman connects properly, and gets a four, everyone applauds. If he gets a **nick** and gets **caught behind** by the wicket keeper or the slips (see page 53) everyone tends to say what a terrible and irresponsible shot it was!

Some batsmen are naturally more attacking than others. Also, batsmen will become more attacking, or more defensive, depending on the state of the match. However, the sort of shot that the batsman plays will normally depend largely upon the sort of ball that the bowler bowls.

We therefore look next at how the bowler tends to bowl.

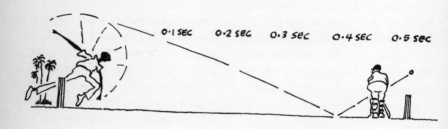

Bowling

Fast Bowlers

Some bowlers are called **fast**. At top level this means that they deliver the ball at a speed of around 90 mph. This is 44 yards per second. Since the ball is delivered at a distance of slightly less than 22 yards from the batsman he has slightly less than half a second, after delivery, before the ball has passed him.

In fact, of course, the batsman has much less time than this after the ball has bounced off the pitch.

Bowling Not Throwing

This makes it crucial that the bowler should deliver the ball with his bowling arm kept straight just before and during final delivery. In this way, the batsman can begin to judge the **line** of the delivery from the arc of the bowler's arm. He can also begin to judge where the ball is likely to bounce by noting when the bowler releases the ball as his arm comes over. The later that the bowler releases the ball the sooner, and further from the batsman, it will bounce. A top batsman uses these clues to anticipate where the ball is likely to go.

If the bowler throws the ball, by straightening his arm as he delivers, the batsman has much less chance of judging the **line** and **length** (see page 41). A throw is called as a no ball (see page 47).

Fast Medium Bowlers

Most Test match bowlers are called **fast medium**. They rely on **line** and **length**. They also try to make the ball **swing** (through the air) and/or **seam** (deviate in line after bouncing). We shall now look at each of these factors in turn.

LINE

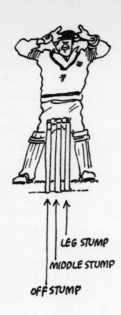

LEG STUMP

MIDDLE STUMP

OFF STUMP

LENGTH

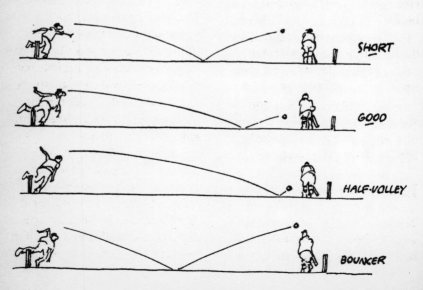

SHORT

GOOD

HALF-VOLLEY

BOUNCER

Bowling

Line

The line of the ball may be outside the off stump; on the off stump; on the middle stump; on the leg stump; or outside the leg stump. (If the ball is too wide for the batsman to play it is called a **wide**; and the batting side is given an extra run as a penalty to the bowler).

Most Test match bowlers bowl a line on or just outside the off stump. This is sometimes called the **corridor of uncertainty** for the batsman. The batsman must avoid the ball hitting the wicket (and thus being out, bowled); equally he must avoid playing at the ball and merely getting an **edge** which may be **caught behind**.

(If a fielder catches a hit off the bat, or the batsman's hand, before the ball has bounced, the batsman is **out, caught**).

If the ball is clearly not **on the wicket** the batsman has the choice of whether to leave it or whether to play an attacking shot.

Length

The length of the ball describes where it bounces. A **good length ball** is one that leaves the batsman uncertain as to whether to play forward or back.

If the ball is **too short** the batsman has time to see it after it has bounced; and he may therefore have time to pull it (to leg) or cut it (to off).

If the ball is **over-pitched** it may be a half-volley which the batsman can drive. (However, if the ball is pitched up a little further, so it lands on or very near the batting crease, it then becomes difficult to play. This ball is called a **yorker**).

Extremes of Length

At one extreme, the ball may be so short-pitched as to become a **bouncer** (which might hit the batsman's head or upper body; be dodged or ducked by the batsman; or be hooked by the batsman). A very short ball that does not bounce high is called a **long hop**; and it will get clouted!

At the other extreme, a fast full toss that is directed at the batsman's head or upper body is called a **beamer**. The beamer is illegal because the batsman does not expect it and it could hurt him seriously (or even kill him if it hit

COULD KILL HIM

YORKER

Bowling

him on the temple). A cricket ball is very hard and it weighs approximately 160g (just under six ounces).

Swing

Normal swing (through the air) depends upon the fact that a cricket ball (when **new**) has a shiny surface but a pronounced seam. If the ball is delivered with the seam upright, but at an angle, air flows across the two surfaces in different ways and makes the ball move sideways through the air.

Swing is still not fully understood. The bowler's grip on the ball and his delivery action both have an effect. The atmospheric conditions can also be crucial. The ball tends to swing much more in moist conditions. Even cloud cover can have a crucial effect.

There also appears to be an optimum speed at which swing occurs. A fast bowler can sometimes achieve more swing by bowling a little slower.

Reverse swing is a new phenomenon. Some people suggest it is based on making one side of the ball heavier than the other; by allowing one side to become wet whilst the other is kept dry. Others suggest it can occur if one side of the ball becomes scuffed up whilst the other remains smooth and shiny. Both may have an effect.

The fielders are not allowed to scuff the ball deliberately or, indeed, to **pick the seam** in order to raise it. This is called **ball tampering**.

Seam

The ball may deviate off the pitch if it lands on the seam of the ball (which protrudes). This technique is particularly effective on many English pitches which are often slightly damp and soft. This enables the ball to **dig in**.

OFFSPIN

LEG SPIN

Bowling

Spin Bowlers

Some bowlers are **spinners**. They bowl more slowly and from shorter run-ups.

Off-spin bowlers make the ball spin into the right-handed batsman after pitching on the offside.

The deliveries are called **off-breaks**. This method of spinning is also called **finger spin**.

Leg-spin bowlers *make* the ball spin away from the right-handed batsman after pitching, perhaps, on middle or leg stump.

The deliveries are called **leg breaks**. This method of spinning is also called **wrist spin.**

By retaining the same action, but altering the position of his wrist, a leg-spinner may be able to produce a **top-spinner** (which **shoots** quickly, and straight, when it pitches) or a **googly** (which comes back into the batsman, unexpectedly, like an off-break. The googly is also called a **wrong-un**; for obvious reasons.

Finger spinners are generally more accurate than wrist spinners; but spin the ball less.

Spin bowlers do not rely entirely (or sometimes even mainly) on spin.

They are also able to **flight** the ball. They have a knack of making the ball **loop** down just before it bounces. This deceives the batsman into thinking that the ball has been over-pitched and can safely be driven.

Bowling is complicated by the fact that a bowler can be left-handed instead of right-handed.

Left-arm spinners are actually quite common. They have an off-break action; but the ball spins away from a right-handed batsman (as would a leg-break from a right-handed bowler).

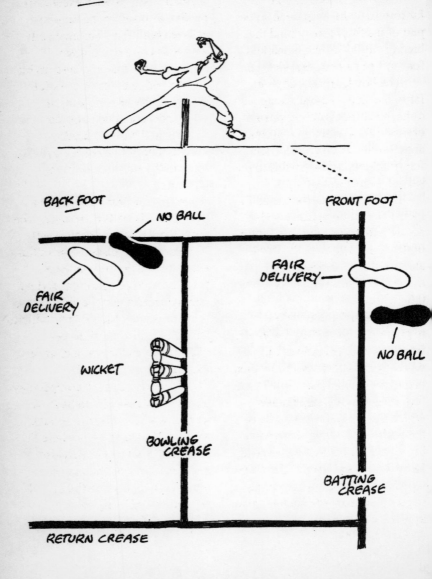

THE DELIVERY

BACK FOOT

NO BALL

FAIR DELIVERY

FAIR DELIVERY

FRONT FOOT

NO BALL

WICKET

BOWLING CREASE

BATTING CREASE

RETURN CREASE

The Delivery

The bowler has to deliver the ball from near the non-striker's wicket.

The bowler must not go too far forward – he must keep some part of his front foot behind the batting crease (which is marked four feet in front of the wicket).

The bowler must not go too far to the side – he must keep all of his back foot within a **return crease** (which is marked at right angles to the batting crease and four feet [less half an inch!] to the side of the nearest stump).

(Don't worry about the half an inch! The batting crease is also actually four feet from the centre of the stumps and not the front; and the stumps must have a minimum radius of approximately 0.6 inches!)

Until 1970, there was no restriction at all on the bowler's front foot and he could put it where he liked. However, he then had to have some part of this back foot behind a **bowling crease** which ran through the middle of the wicket. Nowadays the bowling crease serves no real purpose. However, it is always still marked – perhaps for tradition or perhaps to guide the groundsman on where to place the stumps!

No ball

If either of the bowler's feet is in the wrong position the umpire calls **no ball.** This automatically counts as one extra unless:

- the batsman manages to hit the ball and, instead, scores one or more runs himself;
- additional no balls are credited because a larger number of byes or leg byes would otherwise have re-sulted.

A no ball does not count as one of the six balls in an over. The bowler has to bowl another ball.

Nor can the batsman be out to a no ball (except run out when actually attempting to run, and not merely standing out of his ground; or under some obscure laws which basically deal with improper interference in the conduct of the game).

You might think it complicates things for the umpire to have to look at where the bowler's back foot has landed; then at where the bowler's front foot has landed; and then down the pitch to see what has happened to the ball. If so, you would be right!

OVER THE WICKET

ROUND THE WICKET

The Delivery

A bowler can also be no balled for other reasons:

- for bowling a beamer or persistent bouncers (unfair play);
- because the wicket-keeper or a fielder is in an illegal position;
- for throwing (i.e. straightening his arm during his delivery). This is most unlikely to occur during an international match.

Wide Ball

A wide ball is one that passes the wicket out of reach of the batsman (standing in a normal position).

One extra is scored (or whatever larger number of byes would otherwise have resulted). A wide ball does not count as one of the six balls in an over; another must be bowled.

Over and Round the Wicket

The bowler is allowed to bowl from either side of the wicket.

The more 'natural' side is where the bowler has his chest to the wicket rather than his back. Where the bowler has his chest to the wicket he is said to be bowling **over the wicket**.

Where the bowler has his back to the wicket he is said to be bowling **round the wicket**.

Notice that over and round the wicket will mean different sides of the wicket for a right-arm bowler and a left-arm bowler.

Maiden Over

A **maiden** over is one in which no runs are scored (and which contains no wides or no balls). If the bowler also takes a wicket, the over is called a **wicket maiden**.

A bowler's full analysis is normally given as overs; maidens; runs; wickets. The number of maidens has no real significance and it is difficult to see why so much attention is given to this. When a bowler's figures are summarised only the wickets and runs are given (in the reverse order)!

So, if Smith's full figures are 20 overs; 4 maidens; 40 runs; 5 wickets this will be summarised as 'Smith took 5 for 40'. One might then add 'off 20 overs'.

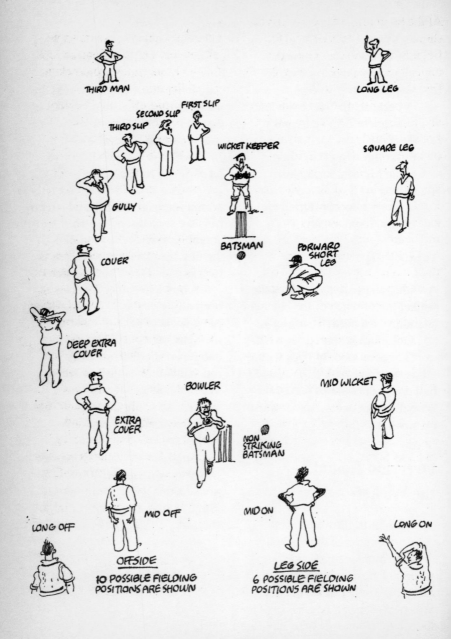

Fielding

At the beginning of each over you should look to see where all the fielders are standing. Once you understand the pattern you will find this quite easy to do.

There will always be a bowler and there will always be a wicket keeper. This leaves exactly nine other players who are fielding.

The first thing to note is the split between the offside and the legside. Are they split 6-3; 5-4; or even 4-5? (Occasionally you might even see a 7-2 field).

The next thing to note is what their main purposes seem to be.

Fielders are placed with three purposes in mind:
- to take catches;
- to save singles;
- to save boundaries.

It is best to start by looking at field settings for the traditional version of the game. In limited-overs' games there are some special restrictions on where the fielders can stand.

NOTE:
In the illustration opposite some possible fielding positions are not shown because they would clutter up the diagram.

Silly mid off would be very close to, and in front of, the batsman but on the other side of the pitch from forward short leg.

Point would be square to the batsman on the offside (and therefore between gully and cover).

Long stop would stand directly behind the wicket keeper (in case he misses the ball) but this is not considered necessary in top class cricket! At lower levels of cricket long leg is often placed at **fine leg** – which is midway between long stop and long leg.

Leg slip would stand close behind the batsman on the leg side. However, no more than two fielders are allowed to stand behind the batsman on the leg side. This is to discourage excessive legside (**bodyline**) bowling.

LONG LEG

THIRD SLIP

SECOND SLIP

FIRST SLIP

WICKET KEEPER

GULLY

COVER

BATSMAN

FORWARD SHORT LEG

EXTRA COVER

BOWLER

NON STRIKING BATSMAN

MID WICKET

ATTACKING FIELD
TO RIGHT HANDED BATSMAN

OFFSIDE
6

LEGSIDE
3

Fielding

Traditional – Attacking Field

At the start of a Test match you might see a 6-3 field. (This means, remember, that six fielders are on the offside and three are on the legside).

In the opening stages of the game, the fast, or fast medium, bowlers will be bowling with a hard and shiny new ball (which may swing and bounce a lot). The main hope of the fielding side is that the **opening batsmen** will **get an edge** to the wicket-keeper; or to one of the **slip-fielders** (or **slips**) who stand to the side of the wicket-keeper.

Typically, therefore, the match may begin with the fielding side perhaps having three slips and **a gulley**; all in **close catching** positions hoping for an edge.

The gulley stands rather wider than the slips. (Gulley is a specialist position because the ball will come more off the **face of the bat** than the edge. It may therefore come to the fielder more slowly, if the shot has been defensive; or more quickly if the shot has been attacking).

The two other fielders on the offside tend to stand at **cover** and **extra cover**. They are there mainly to prevent the batsman from **pushing** singles to the offside.

On the legside there is (almost) always a fielder at **long leg**. He stops glances from going to the boundary (which would count as four runs). However, to be in a position to stop the fours, he will have to be **deep** enough to permit the batsman to **take a single** to him. Long leg may also be able to stop, or even catch, a hook shot.

To begin with, another fielder (with a helmet) will probably crouch very close to the batsman at **forward short leg**. He is there to catch the ball if it touches the bat and rebounds off the batsman's pads.

Finally, one fielder tends to be placed at **mid wicket**. He has to run after any balls that are driven; flicked; or pulled to the legside. Very few are, if the bowler is bowling accurately at the off stump area.

THIRD MAN

LONG LEG

FIRST SLIP

WICKET KEEPER

DEEP
SQUARE LEG

GULLY

BATSMAN

COVER

BOWLER

MID WICKET

EXTRA
COVER

NON
STRIKING
BATSMAN

MID OFF

DEFENSIVE FIELD
TO RIGHT HANDED BATSMAN

OFFSIDE
6

LEGSIDE
3

— 54 —

Fielding

Traditional – Defensive Field

In due course the field placings will normally become more defensive as each of the batsmen gets his eye in.

Third slip may be taken out and dropped back into the outfield at third man; where his job is to stop boundaries.

Second slip might be moved to deep extra cover, behind the cover fielders, to save fours. Alternatively, he might be moved to mid off or mid on to stop the batsman from driving. (If he moves across to mid on, the 6-3 field will become a 5-4 field).

Forward short leg might be moved back to square leg.

If a spinner is bowling, mid off (or mid on) may be moved further back to long off (or long on).

In a Test match, the fielding side are entitled to have a second new ball after 85 overs have been bowled (by which time the old ball will have become worn and relatively soft).

When the new ball is taken some of the fielders may move back into attacking, close catching positions.

THE PLAYING FIELD AND THE 'CIRCLE'

(TO SCALE)

BOUNDARY

Fielding

Limited-Overs

In the early days of limited-overs' games, captains realised that they could slow down the batting side by putting most of the fielders around the boundary. Because the innings was limited by the maximum number of overs, taking wickets didn't matter as much as stopping runs. This made for boring games; so fielding restrictions were introduced.

In limited-overs' games there is a '**circle**' 30 yards from the wicket. (It is actually a lozenge formed by two semi-circles, around each wicket, joined by two straight lines).

A minimum of four fielders (in addition to the wicket-keeper and the bowler) must be inside the circle when the bowler bowls. Otherwise a no ball will be called.

In addition, there is (sometimes) an extra restriction for the first 15 overs of each innings. The minimum inside the circle is then seven fielders. In other words, only two fielders can be outside the circle for the first 15 overs. (This is intended to encourage the opening batsman to take the risk of hitting out early on when the fielders are almost all close in).

It will be seen that the purpose of these restrictions is to force teams to set fields that are fairly similar to those set in traditional games.

Out

There are ten ways of getting out in cricket (but some of them are very rare). Let's first summarise the main ways of getting out.

As we saw from the start, a batsman can be **caught** and he can be **run out**. The batsman is caught if a fielder catches the ball off the bat (or the batsman's hand when holding the bat) before it touches the ground. The batsman is run out if a fielder breaks the wicket with the ball (or his hand when holding the ball) when the batsman is out of his ground.

We then saw that being **bowled** was one of the important differences between cricket and baseball (or rounders). The batsman is bowled if the bowler delivers the ball fairly and it breaks the wicket (dislodges a bail).

There is a variation on being bowled which we have not yet considered.

The game would not make much sense if the batsman could prevent himself from being bowled merely by standing in front of his wicket and letting every ball hit his pads.

To avoid this, the batsman can be out **leg-before-wicket (lbw)** if he uses any part of this body (except his hand, see below) to prevent himself from being bowled.

However, there are some restrictions on lbw and, in some cases where the ball would have hit the wicket, the batsman is given **not out**. These restrictions seem quite logical when the reasons are explained.

The batsman cannot be out lbw if the ball pitched (or hit the batsman) outside the line of his leg stump. This is mainly to discourage right-arm bowlers from bowling round the wicket at the batsman's body. This bowling tactic can make for boring and/or dangerous cricket.

The batsman is also not out lbw if he has made a genuine attempt to play the ball *and* he is not directly between the line of the wickets (which are only nine inches wide, remember) at the moment of impact.

Notice that the batsman loses this immunity if he has not attempted to play a shot; but has merely **padded up** outside the line of his off stump.

The batsman is also not out lbw if he has hit the ball with his bat before it hits his body.

The batsman's hand counts as part of the bat if it is holding bat. (If the hand is not holding the bat the batsman may be out for handling the ball, and not lbw, see below).

Notice how the law tries to restrict the scope of lbw to cases which are fairly blatant. Despite this, batsmen often grumble about lbw decisions. (TV replays sometimes seem to back them up – but these can be misleading because the camera is usually slightly off centre and the camera foreshortens the distances). There is an old retort to a batsman who complains about an lbw decision – if you were so sure where the ball was, why didn't you hit it?

These are the four most common methods of dismissal. One other occurs from time to time.

The batsman is **stumped** if he is out of his ground whilst receiving the ball and the wicket-keeper (directly) breaks the wicket (in the normal way).

The following method of dismissal is fairly rare.

The batsman is out, **hit wicket**, if he breaks the wicket himself whilst receiving the ball (or preparing to receive the ball; or setting off for his first run).

In all of the above cases, except run out, the bowler is credited, individually, with having taken the wicket.

Four other methods of dismissal hardly ever (or never) occur. These are **handling the ball; hitting the ball twice** (except to protect the wicket); **obstructing the field**; and **timed out** (i.e. wilfully not coming out to bat within two minutes of the fall of a wicket). To date, no one has ever been timed out in a Test match. In none of these four latter cases does the bowler get any individual credit for the wicket.

Howzat!

Strictly speaking the batsman is not out unless an **appeal** is made to the umpire by a member of the fielding side. The fielders normally shout "Howzat!" (i.e. "How is that?") or sometimes "Howzee!" (i.e. "How is he?").

In practice a batsman will normally **walk** without waiting for an appeal if he has been bowled. It is also sporting to walk if the batsman knows he has edged a catch behind the wicket.

Ducks and Golden Ducks

A batman who is out for no runs has scored a **duck**. If the batsman is out first ball he has got a **golden duck**.

Test Matches

A Test match is played over five days. On each day there are normally three **sessions** each of two hours. There is the **morning session;** the **afternoon session;** and the **after-tea session.** They are all split by the **lunch interval** (40 minutes) and the **tea interval** (20 minutes).

A minimum number of (six ball) overs has to be bowled in the day. Currently this is 90 overs. (The overs are bowled from alternate ends and no one can bowl two successive overs).

Each side has two **innings**. The two captains toss a coin for choice of first innings. The side that wins the toss normally bats first. (It is galling to put the opposition in, thinking the pitch will favour bowlers early on, then watch them make a huge score). A side is bowled out when it has lost ten wickets. The captain may declare an innings closed if he thinks he has got enough runs and wants time to bowl out the other side.

If (in the first innings) the side batting second score 200 less runs than the side batting first the second side may be 'asked' to follow on. They must then start their second innings immediately after their first innings has ended.

A side wins if it has scored more runs after the opposing side has completed its two innings. Notice

that the winning side can win either by so many wickets (if it is batting last) or by so many runs (if it is bowling last).

Notice also that a side cannot lose unless it has completed two innings. (A declaration counts as a completed innings.) A game can end in a draw; and Test matches quite often do.

However, drawn games can still be exciting if the result is in the balance for much of the game. Even if one side is well on top, the other side may be able to hang on for a draw. Moreover, the possibility of a drawn can encourage the stronger side to quicken its scoring rate and/or declare in order to give more time to get the opposition out.

What is a good score in a Test match?

It all depends, but the scoring rate in Test matches now rarely goes much above three runs an over during the entire game. The game lasts for five days, with 90 overs being bowled per day. In total, therefore, the game will last for a maximum of 450 overs.

This will produce 1,350 runs if the scoring rate is maintained at three runs per over. Let's say 1,300 runs (not least because, in practice, a few overs will be lost when the teams change innings etc).

It follows that if a side can score more than 650 runs in its two innings it should not normally expect to lose. For this reason, the side batting first likes to make a score of 400, perhaps 500, or even 600 in its first innings. If it can achieve this its chances of losing are increasingly slim.

However, if the side is, say 280 for 3 wickets at the end of the first day's play it will reckon to pass 400 sometime after lunch on the second day. Working further backwards, if a side is 190 for 1 wicket at tea on the first day, it will certainly hope to reach 280 by close of play without losing too many wickets. Finally, it is very nice to be 90, or so, for 0 wicket at lunch on the first day.

The first one or two sessions of play in a Test match may therefore sometimes have a decisive effect on the remaining course of the game. However, that is not to say that sudden and unexpected batting collapses never occur!

Another factor can sometimes be important. A Test match pitch can deteriorate over five days of play and may increasingly favour a particular bowler. In addition there are sometimes huge psychological pressures on the side which bats last.

No team really likes to face a target of much over 200 in the fourth innings; and there have been some famous defeats when the target was less than 150.

One famous occasion was at Headingley (Leeds) in 1981 when England played Australia. After interruptions for bad light, Australia ended the first day at 210 for 3. On the second day, Australia declared at 401 for 9 to make England bat for two overs before close of play. By tea on the third day, England were all out for 174 (227 runs behind). England were made to follow on and lost a wicket before bad light again stopped play. On the afternoon of the fourth day, England were reduced to 135 for 7, still 92 runs behind and facing an innings defeat. However, the last three England wickets (quite improbably) took the score to 356 all out. Ian Botham made 149 not out. On the last day, Australia needed just 130 runs to win. Bob Willis then took 8 wickets for 43 runs and Australia were all out for 111. England therefore won one of the most extraordinary matches ever played by 18 runs. At one stage, the book-makers had quoted England as 500–1 against – and, for a joke, some of the Australian players had placed bets!

Limited-Overs' Internationals (LOI's)

In these games, both sides have just one innings which is restricted to a set number of overs (in internationals, currently normally 50). The side that scores the most runs wins.

There are restrictions on the bowlers; no bowler can bowl more than one-fifth of the maximum number of his side's overs.

There are also special restrictions which prevent too many fielders from being posted around the boundary to stop fours. A 'circle' is marked 30 yards from the wickets. For the first 15 overs, seven fielders (in addition to the wicket-keeper and the bowler) must remain inside it. For the remaining overs, four fielders must remain inside it.

In limited-overs' games, the batting side initially tries to score briskly while keeping wickets in hand. Then, over the last 10-15 overs, the batsmen tend to hit out as much as they can.

A good score in a limited- overs' game will depend a lot on the condition of the pitch (and even the size of the ground). Off 50 overs, a good score might be around 250, give or take 25.

In England, for example, there are three major limited-overs' competitions played each year. The oldest is a knock-out competition. There is also a Sunday league (in which the teams wear coloured clothing).

In some other countries, limited-overs' games are often played as **day/night** matches. The first inning is played during the afternoon – in daylight. The second innings is played in the evening – under floodlights. A white ball has to be used; which makes coloured clothing essential.

Day/night games are becoming increasingly popular around the world (at those grounds that can afford the expense of installing floodlighting). However, the English grounds are all at latitudes between 50° and 55° North. They are too light on summer evenings and normally too cold and wet during the rest of the year. (For comparison with England, Auckland, in New Zealand, lies at 38° South. Cape Town, in South Africa, lies in 34° South. The other Test-playing countries are all nearer the Equator).

Other Limited-Overs' Games

Limited-overs' games have also become popular in domestic cricket.

Other Innovations

TV Replays

Where facilities are available, TV replays are now used to judge run-outs, stumpings, and whether or not the ball crossed the boundary.

The umpire calls for this facility by outlining the sides of a box with his two index fingers!

In some systems, the umpire is told the answer by radio. In other systems, a green or red light comes on to show whether the batsman is in or out. Amusingly, the first two experiments with lights had the red and green lights meaning exactly the opposite? Should green mean 'go out' or 'go on batting'? Should red mean 'stop batting' or 'stop at the crease'? (The answer depends on whether you originally envisaged having a third, amber, light to say the TV set had broken down – an idea swiftly abandoned. Since amber then implied 'stop at the crease' so, by analogy with traffic lights, did red).

Match Referees

The International Cricket Council now appoints a match referee (normally a well-known former player) to be in charge of discipline at international matches.

The referee can fine or suspend players for misconduct (including slow play).

International Umpires

In 1994, following some pilot schemes, the International Cricket Council formed the National Grid International Panel of Umpires.

At least one umpire from the panel, from a country not involved in the game, now officiates at every Test match.

Sponsorship

Cricket has attracted a growing amount of commercial sponsorship. Sponsors' names can be seen around the ground and on the players' clothing and equipment. The sponsors give a lot of financial support to the game.

Happy Watching!

Now you've read this book, you should have a good idea of what the game is all about.

You may find it helpful to skim through it again to refresh your memory.

Make sure that you take the book with you to the ground.

The short section about the scoreboard should be useful at the beginning of the day.

Then keep a marker in the section about the fielders. At the beginning of each over, try to make a point of looking to see how the field is set. Is it 6–3 or 5–4 or what?

Otherwise just dip in if you've forgotten something.

Finally, don't be frightened to ask your neighbour if you are not sure about something. Most cricket spectators love explaining the game to other people.

Happy watching!

— 64 —